# *Classic*
# INDIAN

# *Classic*
# INDIAN

*Easy, delicious and authentic recipes*

FOREWORD BY
## RAFI FERNANDEZ

SMITHMARK

© 1996 Anness Publishing Limited

This edition published in 1996 by
SMITHMARK Publishers, a division of US Media Holdings, Inc
16 East 32nd Street
New York NY 10016
USA

SMITHMARK books are available for bulk purchase for sales promotion and for premium use. For details write or call
the Manager of Special Sales, SMITHMARK Publishers, 16 East 32nd Street, New York, NY 10016; (212) 532–6600.

Produced by Anness Publishing Limited
1 Boundary Row
London SE1 8HP

ISBN 0-8317-7369-3

*Publisher* Joanna Lorenz
*Senior Cookery Editor* Linda Fraser
*Cookery Editor* Anne Hildyard
*Designer* Nigel Partridge
*Illustrations* Madeleine David
*Photographers* Edward Allwright, David Armstrong, Steve Baxter and Michael Michaels
*Recipes* Roz Denny, Rafi Fernandez, Sarah Gates, Shehzad Husain,
Deh-Ta Tsiung and Steven Wheeler
*Food for photography* Shehzad Husain, Wendy Lee and Steven Wheeler
*Stylists* Maria Kelly and Blake Minton
*Jacket photography* Amanda Heywood

Typeset by MC Typeset Ltd, Rochester, Kent
Printed and bound in China

Picture on frontispiece: Zefa Pictures Ltd.
Pictures on pages 7, 8 & 9: Michael Busselle

# CONTENTS

# FOREWORD

The birth of classic cuisine in my country can be traced to necessity – that great mother of invention. Early settlers, seeking some way of preserving their food, discovered a large family of ingredients which would not only fulfil that function, but would also promote good health and pep up the appetite. These amazing ingredients were spices. Blending them soon became an art form: achieving the perfect proportions played a very important role in the development of classic Indian dishes.

India is a vast country, and it is not surprising that regions have evolved their own dishes. My country's food reflects the heritage of its peoples, embracing historical developments, religious beliefs, and cultural practices. India has been influenced by many countries, absorbing aspects of their cooking along with their culture, but the unifying factor is the way that fragrant herbs and spices are blended to create dishes that are flavorsome, intriguing, and addictive.

Recipes are handed down from generation to generation, often learned not from books but passed by word of mouth.

Curry (the word originates from the Tamil *kaari*) simply means gravy with extra ingredients like meat, poultry, fish, seafood, legumes and many different vegetables.

Although the first commercial curry powder was invented in Madras in the early part of the nineteenth century, this was largely for export to Britain. Indians prefer to combine their own herbs and spices. The blend, which may be wet or dry, is called masala, and is prepared fresh each day after the menu has been planned. It is this blending of masalas that is the magic of our cuisine – even the humble potato can be transformed in a host of ways depending on the combination of different spices used to make the masala.

This beautifully illustrated book contains some of India's finest classic dishes. The emphasis is on homecooking at its best, and recipes include preparations that have hitherto been the jealously guarded preserve of professionals. I am proud that several of my recipes have been chosen for this collection and wish you good dining or "*Priti Bhojan!*"

RAFI FERNANDEZ

# INTRODUCTION

Indian cooking is renowned for its use of spices, herbs, and flavorings. The dishes of this great sub-continent range from mild creamy kormas to the fiery curries of Madras, but the common denominator is the blending of spices so that each single dish has a distinctive signature, be it subtle or strident.

Indian dishes, even sweetmeats, are seldom cooked without spices. Rubbed into meats, made into masalas (the dry mixes or pastes used for curries), or combined with cream, yogurt, or coconut milk to make rich, smooth sauces, spices are essential to authentic Indian cooking. Try to buy whole spices and grind them yourself, as once spices are ground they lose their flavor and aroma in a relatively short time.

Many Indian dishes, especially those from the south, owe their

*A colorful selection of fruit – an essential refreshment after spicy food (left), the breathtaking splendor of the Taj Mahal (above), and a stall selling a variety of sweet and savory snacks (right), reflect some of the contrasting faces of India.*

fiery flavor to fresh chilies. The seeds are particularly hot, and these may be discarded if you prefer a somewhat milder flavor. Use gloves when preparing chilies, or wash your hands very thoroughly afterwards. Touching delicate skin, especially around the eyes or lips, immediately after handling chilies can cause an unpleasant reaction. Ginger also adds a hint of heat to many dishes. It is a very common ingredient in Indian cooking. Always use the fresh ginger root, rather than ground where this is indicated in recipes.

Other ingredients that frequently feature are fresh fruit and vegetables, dried legumes, rice, and nuts. India has the largest population of vegetarians of any country in the world, and vegetables and grains are often presented as dishes in their own right. Ghee, which is a type of clarified butter, is also used extensively, especially in the north. It has a rich nutty flavor and is good for both shallow and deep-frying.

An Indian meal may consist of a meat or fish dish, one or two vegetable dishes, a dhal (a dish consisting of cooked legumes), a bowl of yogurt, bread and/or rice, and perhaps a salad or a spicy chutney. Indian breads are the perfect vehicle for rich meat or fish

dishes or dhals. However, bread is only served in northern, western, and eastern India; in the south, rice is the more common accompaniment. There are countless ways of cooking rice, and each region adds some-

thing unique by way of flavoring. For everyday cooking, long grain or patna rice is used. When cooked, it should be dry and fluffy. For special dishes, basmati rice is favored for its fine, delicately aromatic, flavor. Indian meals often finish with fresh fruit such as mangoes or guavas. Alternatively, Kulfi, a delicious ice cream, is served (see page 56).

We are fortunate in being able to buy a wide range of spices and traditional Indian ingredients from our supermarkets and ethnic shops today. Whether your preference is for Tandoori Chicken, Lamb Korma, or Spiced Spinach and Potatoes, recreating classic Indian dishes has never been easier, so invest in a few of your favorite spices, turn to any of the delectable recipes in this book, and treat your family and friends to the true taste of India.

# CHICKEN TIKKA

**T**his chicken dish is an extremely popular starter and is quick and easy to cook. It can also be served as a main course for four.

## INGREDIENTS

*1 pound skinless, boneless, chicken breast, cubed*

*1 teaspoon grated fresh ginger root*

*1 garlic clove, crushed*

*1 teaspoon chili powder*

*¼ teaspoon ground turmeric*

*1 teaspoon salt*

*⅔ cup plain yogurt*

*4 tablespoons lemon juice*

*1 tablespoon chopped fresh cilantro*

*1 tablespoon vegetable oil*

*1 small onion, cut into rings, lime wedges, mixed salad and fresh cilantro sprigs, to garnish*

SERVES 6

### COOK'S TIP
Serve Chicken Tikka, hot or cold, as a snack with drinks. Cut into bite-size pieces and serve on toothpicks.

1 In a bowl, mix together the chicken pieces, ginger, garlic, chili powder, turmeric, salt, yogurt, lemon juice, and cilantro. Cover the bowl and leave to marinate for at least 2 hours.

2 Place the chicken pieces in a broiler pan or a flameproof dish lined with foil and brush with the oil.

3 Preheat the broiler to medium. Broil the chicken pieces for 15–20 minutes until cooked, turning and basting 2–3 times. Serve on individual plates, garnished with onion rings, lime wedges, mixed salad and fresh cilantro sprigs.

# SPICED EGGPLANTS

The exact origins of the eggplant are uncertain but it has been cultivated in India since ancient times. It comes from the same family as the potato and is related to both the petunia and the tobacco plant.

INGREDIENTS

*2 eggplants, halved lengthwise*
*salt*
*4 tablespoons olive oil, plus extra if needed*
*2 large onions, thinly sliced*
*2 garlic cloves, crushed*
*1 green bell pepper, seeded and sliced*
*14-ounce can chopped tomatoes*
*3 tablespoons sugar*
*1 teaspoon ground coriander*
*ground black pepper*
*2 tablespoons chopped fresh cilantro or parsley*
*fresh cilantro sprigs, to garnish*
*crusty bread, to serve*

SERVES 4

1 Using a sharp knife, slash the flesh of the eggplants a few times. Sprinkle the eggplants with salt and drain in a colander for about 30 minutes. Rinse well and pat dry.

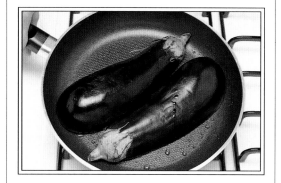

2 Gently fry the eggplants, cut-side down, in the oil for 5 minutes, then drain and place in a shallow ovenproof dish.

3 In the same pan, gently fry the onions, garlic, and green bell pepper, adding extra oil if necessary. Cook for about 10 minutes, stirring occasionally, until all the vegetables have softened.

4 Add the tomatoes, sugar, ground coriander, and black pepper to the onion and green bell pepper mixture. Stir to combine thoroughly, then cook for about 5 minutes until the mixture is reduced. Stir in the chopped cilantro or parsley.

5 Preheat the oven to 375°F. Spoon the mixture on top of the halved eggplants, cover, and bake for 30–35 minutes. Cool, garnish with cilantro sprigs, and serve cold with crusty bread.

COOK'S TIP
Sprinkling the cut surfaces of eggplants with salt allows the juices that form to drain away in a colander. Before cooking, it is important to rinse the eggplants well and pat dry with paper towels. Prepared like this, eggplants are less bitter.

# SPICY KOFTA

**S**erve these tasty meatballs piping hot with naan bread, a raita made with cucumber and plain yogurt, tomato salad, and a spicy relish.

### INGREDIENTS
*1 pound lean ground beef or lamb*
*2 tablespoons grated fresh ginger root*
*2 garlic cloves, crushed*
*4 green chilies, finely chopped*
*1 small onion, finely chopped*
*1 egg*
*½ teaspoon ground turmeric*
*1 teaspoon garam masala*
*2 ounces fresh cilantro, chopped*
*4–6 fresh mint leaves, chopped, or*
*½ teaspoon mint sauce*
*1 potato, about 6 ounces*
*salt*
*vegetable oil, for deep-frying*

*MAKES 20–25*

1 Place the ground beef or lamb in a large bowl with the ginger, garlic, chilies, onion, egg, turmeric, garam masala, fresh cilantro, and mint or mint sauce. Grate the potato into the bowl and season with salt. Knead together to form a soft dough.

2 With your hands, shape the mixture into small meatballs the size of golf balls. Cover and leave to rest for about 25 minutes.

3 In a karahi or large frying pan, heat the oil to medium hot, add the meatballs in small batches and fry for 3–5 minutes until they are golden brown (*left*). Drain the meatballs well and serve immediately.

# ONION BHAJIAS

**B**hajias are a classic Indian snack, like a fritter. The same batter may be used with a wide variety of vegetables, such as shredded carrots. Gram flour is a fine flour made from *channa dhal*. It is available from Indian stores.

### INGREDIENTS
*2 cups gram flour (besan) or*
channa atta
*½ teaspoon chili powder*
*1 teaspoon ground turmeric*
*1 teaspoon baking powder*
*¼ teaspoon asafoetida*
*½ teaspoon each, nigella, fennel, cumin,*
*and onion seeds, coarsely crushed*
*2 large onions, finely sliced*
*2 green chilies, seeded and chopped*
*2 ounces fresh cilantro, chopped*
*cold water, to mix*
*vegetable oil, for deep-frying*
*salt*

*MAKES 20–25*

1 In a bowl, mix together the gram flour or *channa atta*, chili powder, and turmeric. Stir in the baking powder and asafoetida. Add salt to taste, then sift into a large mixing bowl.

2 Add the crushed nigella, fennel, cumin, and onion seeds, the sliced onions, green chilies, and fresh cilantro and toss together well. Very gradually, mix in enough cold water to make a thick batter.

3 Heat enough oil in a karahi or large saucepan for deep-frying. Drop spoonfuls of the mixture into the hot oil and fry until golden brown. Leave enough space to turn the bhajias. Drain well and serve hot.

# SAMOSAS

Traditional samosa pastry takes a lot of time and hard work but filo pastry makes an excellent substitute and is readily available. The samosas can be frozen before or after frying.

### INGREDIENTS
*1 package filo pastry, thawed if frozen, wrapped in a damp dish towel*
*vegetable oil, for deep-frying*

### FOR THE FILLING
*3 large potatoes, boiled and roughly mashed*
*3 ounces frozen peas, boiled and drained*
*⅓ cup canned corn, drained*
*1 teaspoon ground coriander*
*1 teaspoon ground cumin*
*1 teaspoon amchur (dry mango powder)*
*1 small red onion, finely chopped*
*2 green chilies, finely chopped*
*2 tablespoons each chopped fresh cilantro and mint*
*juice of 1 lemon, plus more if needed*
*salt*
*chili sauce, to serve*

*MAKES 30*

1 To make the filling, put the mashed potatoes, peas, corn, ground coriander, cumin, amchur, onion, chilies, fresh cilantro, fresh mint, lemon juice, and salt into a large bowl and mix together until well blended. Taste the mixture and add more lemon juice and salt if necessary.

2 Using one strip of pastry at a time, place 1 tablespoon of the filling mixture at one end. Diagonally fold up the pastry to form an enclosed triangle. Moisten the end of the strip with water; press lightly to secure.

3 Heat the oil in a karahi or large saucepan. Fry the samosas in small batches, turning frequently, until golden brown and crisp. Remove with a slotted spoon and drain on paper towels. Serve hot with chili sauce.

### VARIATION
To make a meat filling, fry 1 sliced onion in 2 tablespoons oil for 5 minutes. Add 2 chopped garlic cloves, 1 tablespoon each chopped fresh ginger root, ground cumin, ground coriander, and salt and fry for about 1–2 minutes. Add 1 pound ground lamb and 3 tablespoons water and brown. Cover the pan and cook for 20–25 minutes, stirring occasionally. Drain off the fat, stir in 2 tablespoons chopped fresh mint, ¼ teaspoon garam masala, and 1 tablespoon lemon juice.

# CHICKEN MULLIGATAWNY

This hearty soup was originally made with *mulla ga tani* or pepper water, a sour, spicy flavoring mixture. It became very popular with the British in India during the days of the Raj. There are several variations.

### INGREDIENTS
*2 pounds boneless, skinless chicken
breasts, cut into pieces*
*2½ cups water*
*6 green cardamom pods*
*2-inch piece cinnamon stick*
*4–6 curry leaves*
*1 tablespoon ground coriander*
*1 teaspoon ground cumin*
*½ teaspoon ground turmeric*
*3 garlic cloves, crushed*
*12 whole peppercorns*
*4 cloves*
*1 onion, finely chopped*
*4 ounces creamed coconut*
*salt*
*juice of 2 lemons*
*deep-fried onions, to garnish*

*SERVES 4–6*

1 Place the chicken pieces in a large saucepan with the measured water, bring to a boil, then cover and simmer for about 20 minutes, until the meat is tender. Skim the surface, then strain, reserving the broth. Set the chicken aside and keep warm.

2 Return the broth to the pan and bring back to a boil. Add all the remaining ingredients and simmer for 10–15 minutes, then strain and return the chicken to the soup. Reheat and serve, garnished with the deep-fried onions.

# TOMATO AND CILANTRO SOUP

**A**lthough soups are not often eaten in India and Pakistan, tomato soups of one kind or another are an exception. This one is excellent on a cold winter's day.

## INGREDIENTS
*1½ pounds tomatoes*
*2 tablespoon vegetable oil*
*1 bay leaf*
*4 scallions, chopped*
*1 teaspoon salt*
*1 garlic clove, crushed*
*1 teaspoon black peppercorns, crushed*
*2 tablespoons chopped fresh cilantro*
*3 cups water*
*1 tablespoon cornstarch*
*2 tablespoons light cream, to garnish*
*(optional)*
*bread, to serve (optional)*

*SERVES 4*

---

### COOK'S TIP
Plum tomatoes are ideal for this recipe but if the only fresh tomatoes available are rather pale and under-ripe, add 1 tablespoon tomato paste to the pan with the chopped tomatoes to enhance the color and flavor of the soup.

---

1 To peel the tomatoes, plunge them into boiling water for 20–30 seconds, then into cold water. When cool, peel off the skins, then chop the tomatoes.

2 Heat the oil in a saucepan and fry the tomatoes, bay leaf, and scallions until soft. Add the salt, garlic, peppercorns, and fresh cilantro, and finally stir in the measured water. Bring to a boil, lower the heat, and simmer for 15–20 minutes.

3 Mix the cornstarch with a little water. Remove the soup from the heat and press through a strainer. Return to the pan, add the cornstarch mixture and stir over gentle heat for about 3 minutes, until the soup is thickened and smooth.

4 To serve, ladle the soup into warmed individual bowls and garnish with a swirl of cream, if using. Serve immediately, with bread, if wished.

# BROILED FISH MASALA

These tasty fish fillets with their spicy coating are very simple to prepare. They are cooked using the minimum of oil, so are a healthy option.

### INGREDIENTS
*4 flatfish fillets, such as plaice, sole, or flounder, about 4 ounces each*

#### FOR THE SPICE MIXTURE
*1 garlic clove, crushed*
*1 teaspoon garam masala*
*1 teaspoon chili powder*
*¼ teaspoon ground turmeric*
*½ teaspoon salt*
*1 tablespoon finely chopped fresh cilantro*
*1 tablespoon vegetable oil*
*2 tablespoons lemon juice*
*grated carrot, tomato quarters, and lime slices, to garnish*

#### SERVES 4

1 Line a flameproof dish or broiler pan with foil. Rinse the fish fillets under cold running water, pat dry with paper towels, and put them into the dish or pan.

2 To make the spice mixture, put the crushed garlic clove and garam masala into a small bowl. Stir in the chili powder, ground turmeric, the salt, and the finely chopped fresh cilantro. Gradually add the vegetable oil, stirring constantly. Add the lemon juice and stir thoroughly to mix, then set the spice mixture aside. Preheat the broiler to very hot.

3 Lower the temperature of the broiler to medium. Using a pastry brush, baste the fish fillets evenly all over with the spice mixture. Grill the fish fillets on each side for about 5 minutes, basting occasionally with the juices that form in the pan, until they are cooked right through.

4 To serve, transfer the fish fillets to a warmed serving platter and make a decorative garnish with the grated carrot, tomato quarters, and lime slices. Serve at once, with naan bread, if you like.

---

#### COOK'S TIP
For a stronger flavor, brush the fish fillets with the spice mixture an hour or so before you broil them to allow the spices to permeate the flesh.

# GLAZED GARLIC SHRIMP

**T**his is a fairly quick and simple dish to prepare. Peeling the shrimp means they absorb maximum flavor from the spice mixture. Reserve a few unpeeled shrimp for the garnish.

### INGREDIENTS
*1 tablespoon vegetable oil*
*3 garlic cloves, roughly chopped*
*3 tomatoes, peeled and chopped*
*½ teaspoon salt*
*1 teaspoon crumbled dried red chilies*
*1 teaspoon lemon juice*
*1 tablespoon mango chutney*
*1 green chili, chopped*
*12–16 cooked jumbo shrimp, peeled*
*4 cooked whole jumbo shrimp, fresh cilantro sprigs, and 2 scallions, chopped, to garnish (optional)*

*SERVES 4*

1 Heat the oil in a saucepan and add the chopped garlic. Lower the heat and add the chopped tomatoes with the salt, the crumbled red chilies, lemon juice, mango chutney, and chopped green chili.

2 Add the peeled shrimp to the spice mixture, then turn up the heat and stir-fry, until the shrimp are heated through.

3 Transfer the shrimp and their sauce to a warmed serving dish. Garnish with the whole shrimp, fresh cilantro sprigs, and scallions, if wished.

### COOK'S TIP
For an everyday meal, substitute smaller shrimp for the jumbo shrimp – allowing about 3–4 ounces per person. Serve with rice and a salad of mixed leaves and herbs.

# SPICY FISH PATTIES

**T**hese tasty fish patties can be made slightly larger and served as fish burgers, or shaped into small balls and served as a cocktail snack.

### INGREDIENTS
*1 pound skinned haddock, coley or cod*
*2 potatoes, boiled and mashed*
*4 scallions, finely chopped*
*4 green chilies, finely chopped*
*2-inch piece fresh ginger root,*
*finely chopped*
*fresh cilantro and mint leaves, chopped*
*2 eggs*
*bread crumbs, for coating*
*vegetable oil, for shallow-frying*
*salt and ground black pepper*
*lemon wedges, to garnish*
*chili sauce or sweet chutney, to serve*

### MAKES 20

1 Place the fish in a lightly greased steamer and cook for 10 minutes, until opaque and cooked through. Remove the steamer from the heat and leave the fish on the steaming tray to cool.

2 Flake the fish with a fork and place in a large bowl. Add the potatoes, scallions, chilies, ginger, cilantro, and mint, seasoning, and 1 egg; mix well. Beat the remaining egg in a shallow bowl.

3 Shape the mixture into patties. Dip the patties in egg, then coat in bread crumbs. Heat the oil and fry the patties, in batches, until brown. Serve with chili sauce or chutney. Garnish with lemon wedges.

# BALTI FISH IN COCONUT SAUCE

**U**se fresh fish fillets to make this dish if you can, as they have much more flavor than frozen ones. If you are using frozen fillets, ensure that they are completely thawed before cooking.

### INGREDIENTS
*2 tablespoons corn oil*
*1 teaspoon onion seeds*
*4 dried red chilies, crumbled*
*3 garlic cloves, sliced*
*1 onion, sliced*
*2 tomatoes*
*2 tablespoons dried coconut*
*1 teaspoon salt*
*1 teaspoon ground coriander*
*4 flatfish fillets, such as plaice, sole, or flounder, about 3 ounces each*
*⅔ cup water*
*1 tablespoon lime juice*
*1 tablespoon chopped fresh cilantro*
*rice or parathas, to serve*

### SERVES 4

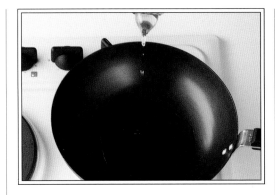

1 Heat the oil in a deep round-bottomed frying pan or a karahi. Lower the heat slightly and add the onion seeds, dried red chilies, garlic, and onion. Cook the mixture for 3–4 minutes, stirring once or twice.

2 Cut a cross on the base of each tomato. Plunge the tomatoes into a bowl of boiling water for 20–30 seconds, then into a bowl of cold water. Peel off the skins, then slice thinly. Add the tomatoes, dried coconut, salt, and ground coriander to the pan and stir to mix thoroughly.

3 Cut each fish fillet into three pieces. Drop the fish pieces into the onion and tomato mixture and turn them gently until they are well coated.

4 Cook for 5–7 minutes, lowering the heat if necessary. Add the measured water, lime juice, and chopped fresh cilantro and cook for another 3–5 minutes, until the water has almost all evaporated. Serve the fish with rice or parathas.

### COOK'S TIP
Balti is the name of both a deep, rounded frying pan with two ring handles, and the dish cooked in it. Also known as a karahi, the Balti pan is very similar to a wok, which makes an excellent substitute.

# SHRIMP AND VEGETABLE KEBABS

This is a light and nutritious dish, excellent served either on a bed of salad leaves, with plain boiled rice, or with whole wheat chapatis.

## INGREDIENTS

2 tablespoons chopped fresh cilantro
1 teaspoon salt
2 green chilies, seeded
and chopped
3 tablespoons lemon juice
2 tablespoons vegetable oil
12 jumbo shrimp, cooked and peeled
1 zucchini, thickly sliced
1 onion, cut into 8 chunks
8 cherry tomatoes
4 baby corn
mixed salad leaves, to serve

*SERVES 4*

---

**COOK'S TIP**
If you are using wooden or bamboo skewers, soak them in cold water before use to prevent them from scorching.

---

1 Place the chopped cilantro, salt, green chilies, lemon juice, and oil in a food processor or blender, and process for a few seconds until blended.

2 Transfer the cilantro mixture to a bowl and add the shrimp. Stir thoroughly to make sure that all the shrimp are well coated. Cover the bowl and set aside in a cool place to marinate for about 30 minutes. Preheat the broiler to very hot.

3 Turn the temperature of the broiler down to medium. Arrange the vegetables and shrimp alternately on four skewers. Place the skewers under the preheated broiler for 5–7 minutes, frequently basting with any remaining marinade, until the vegetables and shrimp are cooked and lightly browned on all sides.

4 Serve the kebabs immediately on a bed of mixed salad leaves.

# TANDOORI CHICKEN

**T**his is a popular Indian chicken dish, which is cooked in a clay oven called a tandoor. Although the authentic tandoori flavor is very difficult to achieve in conventional ovens, this version still makes an exceedingly tasty dish.

INGREDIENTS

*4 chicken quarters*
*¾ cup plain yogurt*
*1 teaspoon garam masala*
*1 teaspoon grated fresh ginger root*
*1 garlic clove, crushed*
*1½ teaspoon chili powder*
*¼ teaspoon ground turmeric*
*1 teaspoon ground coriander*
*1 tablespoon lemon juice*
*1 teaspoon salt*
*few drops of red food coloring*
*2 tablespoons corn oil*
*mixed salad leaves and lime wedges,*
*to garnish*

SERVES 4

1 Skin and rinse the chicken quarters, then pat dry on paper towels. Make two slits in the flesh of each chicken quarter, place in a dish, and set aside.

2 Mix together the yogurt, garam masala, ginger, garlic, chili powder, turmeric, coriander, lemon juice, salt, red food coloring, and oil and beat together well.

3 Cover the chicken quarters with the spice mixture and leave to marinate for about 3 hours.

4 Preheat the oven to its hottest setting. Transfer the chicken pieces to an ovenproof dish. Bake in the preheated oven for 20–25 minutes, or until the chicken is cooked right through and browned on top.

5 Remove the chicken from the oven, transfer to a serving dish, and garnish with the salad leaves and lime wedges.

28

# CHICKEN IN A CASHEW SAUCE

This chicken dish has a deliciously thick and nutty sauce, and is best served with plain boiled rice. Cashews grow profusely in southern India and are widely used in cooking.

### INGREDIENTS
2 onions
2 tablespoons tomato paste
½ cup cashews
1½ teaspoon garam masala
1 garlic clove, crushed
1 teaspoon chili powder
1 tablespoon lemon juice
¼ teaspoon ground turmeric
1 teaspoon salt
1 tablespoon plain yogurt
2 tablespoons corn oil
1 tablespoon chopped fresh cilantro
1 tablespoon golden raisins
1 pound skinless, boneless chicken breasts, cut into pieces
6 ounces button mushrooms
1¼ cups water
1 tablespoon chopped fresh cilantro, to garnish

### SERVES 4

1 Cut the onions into quarters and place in a food processor or blender. Process for about 1 minute.

2 Add the tomato paste, cashews, garam masala, garlic, chili powder, lemon juice, turmeric, salt, and yogurt and process for another 1–1½ minutes.

3 Heat the oil in a saucepan and pour in the spice mixture. Fry for 2 minutes over medium to low heat. Add the cilantro, golden raisins, and chicken and stir-fry the mixture for 1 minute.

4 Add the mushrooms, pour in the water, and bring to a simmer. Cover the saucepan and cook over low heat for about 10 minutes. Check that the chicken is cooked through and the sauce is thick. Cook for a little longer, if necessary.

5 To serve, ladle the chicken and its sauce on to a warmed serving dish. Garnish with the chopped cilantro.

# CHICKEN BIRYANI

This is a classic dish for important occasions, and is truly fit for royalty. Serve it on a wide, shallow platter for maximum effect.

### INGREDIENTS

*3–3½ pounds skinless, boneless chicken breasts, cut into large pieces*
*4 tablespoons biryani masala paste*
*2 green chilies, chopped*
*1 tablespoon grated fresh ginger root*
*2 garlic cloves, crushed*
*2 ounces fresh cilantro, chopped*
*6–8 fresh mint leaves, chopped*
*⅔ cup plain yogurt*
*4 onions, sliced, deep-fried, and crushed*
*2½ cups basmati rice, washed*
*1 teaspoon black cumin seeds*
*2-inch piece cinnamon stick*
*6 green cardamom pods*
*vegetable oil, for shallow frying*
*4 large potatoes, peeled and quartered*
*1¼ cups skim milk*
*few saffron strands, infused in milk*
*salt*
*2 tablespoons ghee or sweet butter, plus extra for shallow-frying,*
*½ cup cashews and ⅓ cup golden raisins, to garnish*

*Serves 4–6*

1 Mix the chicken with the next nine ingredients in a large bowl, cover, and leave to marinate for about 2 hours. Place in a large heavy pan and cook gently for about 10 minutes. Set aside.

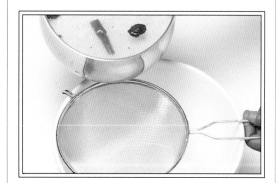

2 Boil a large pan of water. Add the rice with the cumin seeds, cinnamon stick, and cardamom pods; soak for 5 minutes. Drain well. Remove the whole spices.

3 Heat the oil for shallow-frying and fry the potatoes until they are evenly browned on all sides. Drain and set aside.

4 Arrange half of the rice on top of the chicken pieces in the saucepan in an even layer, then make another even layer with the potatoes. Put the remaining rice on top of the potatoes and spread it out to make an even layer.

5 Sprinkle the skim milk all over the rice. Make random holes through the rice with the handle of a spoon and pour a little saffron-flavored milk into each one. Place a few knobs of ghee or butter on the surface of the rice, cover the pan tightly, and cook over low heat for 35–45 minutes.

6 While the biryani is cooking, make the garnish. Heat a little ghee or butter and fry the cashews and golden raisins until they swell. Drain and set aside. When the biryani is ready, gently toss the rice, chicken, and potatoes together. Transfer to a warmed serving platter, garnish with the nut and golden raisin mixture and serve at once.

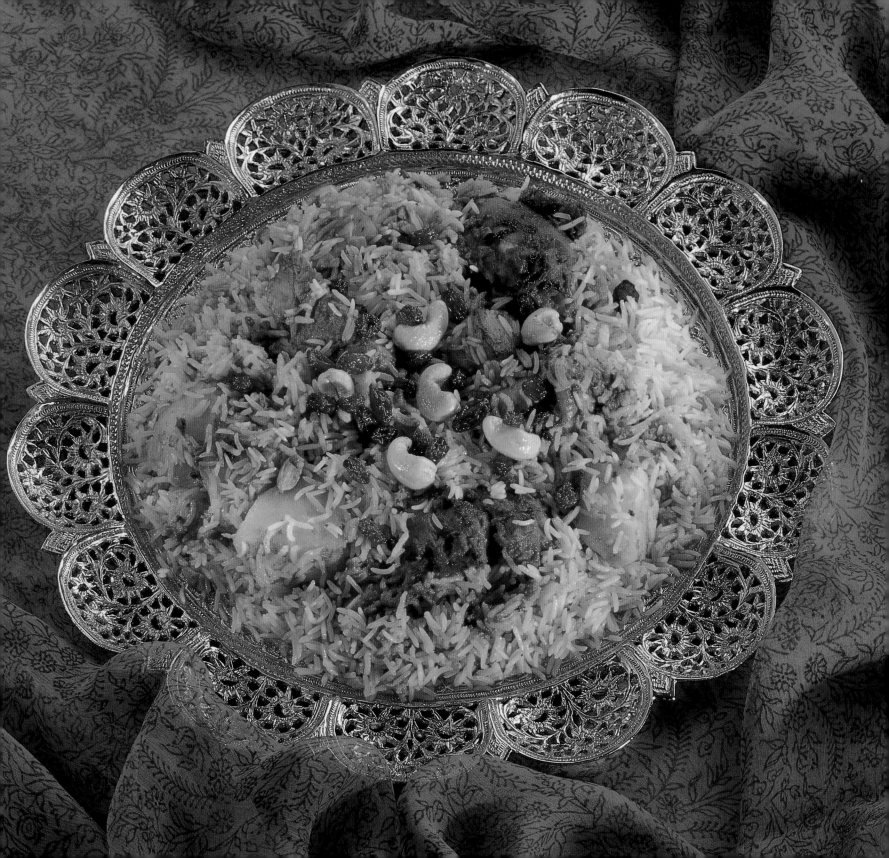

# BEEF WITH GREEN BEANS

Green beans both look and taste good with beef in this aromatic sauce. The sliced red bell pepper used here makes this dish colorful and adds a delicious, sweet touch.

### INGREDIENTS

*10 ounces fine green beans, cut into*
*1-inch pieces*
*2 tablespoons vegetable oil*
*1 onion, sliced*
*1 teaspoon grated fresh ginger root*
*1 garlic clove, crushed*
*1 teaspoon chili powder*
*1¼ teaspoons salt*
*¼ teaspoon ground turmeric*
*2 tomatoes, peeled and chopped*
*1 pound beef, cubed*
*5 cups water*
*1 red bell pepper, sliced*
*1 tablespoon chopped fresh cilantro*
*2 green chilies, chopped*
*whole wheat chapatis, to serve (optional)*

### SERVES 4

1 Cook the green beans in a saucepan of boiling salted water for 5 minutes, then drain and set aside.

2 Heat the oil in a large saucepan and fry the onion until it turns golden brown.

3 Mix together the ginger, garlic, chili powder, salt, turmeric, and chopped tomatoes. Spoon this mixture into the onion and stir-fry for 5–7 minutes.

4 Add the beef and stir-fry for 3 minutes more. Pour in the measured water, bring to a boil, and lower the heat. Cover, and cook for 45 minutes–1 hour, stirring occasionally, until most of the water has evaporated and the meat is tender.

5 Add the green beans to the pan and stir well. Finally, add the sliced red bell pepper, fresh cilantro, and green chilies and cook, stirring constantly, for another 7–10 minutes. Serve hot with whole wheat chapatis, if you like.

# LAMB KORMA

**K**ormas can be very hot indeed but this one is mild, creamy, and aromatic. It comes from the kitchens of the Nizam of Hyderabad.

### INGREDIENTS

*1 tablespoon sesame seeds*
*1 tablespoon white poppy seeds*
*½ cup blanched almonds*
*2 green chilies, seeded*
*6 garlic cloves, sliced*
*2-inch piece fresh ginger root, sliced*
*1 onion, finely chopped*
*3 tablespoons ghee or vegetable oil*
*6 green cardamom pods*
*2-inch piece cinnamon stick*
*4 cloves*
*2 pounds lean lamb, cubed*
*1 teaspoon ground cumin*
*1 teaspoon ground coriander*
*1¼ cups heavy cream*
*½ teaspoon cornstarch*
*salt and ground black pepper*
*roasted sesame seeds, to garnish*

### SERVES 4–6

**1** Heat a heavy-based frying pan and dry-fry the sesame seeds, poppy seeds, almonds, chilies, garlic, ginger, and onion. Cool, then grind finely in a food processor.

**2** Heat the ghee or oil in the frying pan. Fry the cardamom, cinnamon, and cloves until the cloves swell. Add the lamb, cumin, and coriander. Stir in the prepared paste. Season to taste. Cover and cook for 1–1¼ hours, until the lamb is almost done.

**3** Remove the pan from the heat. Mix all but 1 tablespoon of the cream with the cornstarch. Gradually stir into the lamb mixture. Reheat gently, without boiling, and serve, garnished with the sesame seeds and the reserved cream.

# STUFFED EGGPLANTS WITH LAMB

**G**round minced lamb and eggplants go really well together. This is an attractive dish, using different colored bell peppers in the lightly spiced stuffing mixture.

INGREDIENTS

*2 eggplants*

*2 tablespoons vegetable oil*

*1 onion, sliced*

*1 teaspoon grated fresh ginger root*

*1 teaspoon chili powder*

*1 garlic clove, crushed*

*¼ teaspoon ground turmeric*

*1 teaspoon salt*

*1 teaspoon ground coriander*

*1 tomato, chopped*

*12 ounces lean leg of lamb, ground*

*1 green bell pepper, seeded and roughly chopped*

*1 orange bell pepper, seeded and roughly chopped*

*2 tablespoons chopped fresh cilantro*

*½ onion, sliced decoratively, 2 cherry tomatoes, quartered, and fresh cilantro sprigs, to garnish*

*green salad or rice, to serve (optional)*

SERVES 4

1 Preheat the oven to 350°F. Halve the eggplants lengthwise and scoop out most of the flesh and discard. Place the eggplant shells side by side in a large lightly greased ovenproof dish.

2 Heat 1 tablespoon of the oil in a large saucepan and fry the onion for about 5 minutes, stirring occasionally, until golden brown. Gradually stir in the ginger, chili powder, garlic, turmeric, salt, and ground coriander. Add the tomato, lower the heat and stir-fry for 4–5 minutes.

3 Add the ground lamb and continue to stir-fry over medium heat for 7–10 minutes, stirring and turning until the lamb is browned. Add the bell peppers and fresh cilantro to the mixture and stir well.

4 Spoon the lamb mixture into the eggplant shells and brush the edges of the shells with the remaining oil. Bake for 20–25 minutes, until cooked through and browned on top. Garnish with the onion, tomatoes, and cilantro sprigs. Serve with a salad or plain boiled rice, if wished.

# SPICED OKRA WITH ALMONDS

**L**ong and elegantly shaped, it's not surprising these vegetables are commonly called "lady's fingers." Native to tropical Africa, they are very popular in India and Arab countries.

## INGREDIENTS
½ cup blanched almonds, chopped
2 tablespoons butter
8 ounces okra
1 tablespoon sunflower oil
2 garlic cloves, crushed
1-inch piece fresh ginger root, grated
1 teaspoon cumin seeds
1 teaspoon ground coriander
1 teaspoon paprika
1¼ cups water
salt and ground black pepper

*SERVES 2–4*

1 In a shallow flameproof dish, fry the almonds in the butter until they are lightly golden. Remove from the pan with a slotted spoon and drain on paper towels.

2 Using a sharp knife, trim the tops of the okra stems and around the edges of the stalks. The pods contain a sticky liquid which oozes out if they are prepared too far in advance, so trim them just before cooking. Heat the oil in the pan, add the okra and fry, stirring constantly with a wooden spoon, for 2 minutes, until the okra starts to soften.

3 Add the garlic and ginger, and fry gently for 1 minute, then add the cumin seeds, coriander, and paprika and cook for another 1–2 minutes, stirring all the time.

4 Pour in the measured water. Season generously with salt and pepper, cover the pan and simmer for about 5 minutes, until the okra feels just tender when pierced with the tip of a sharp knife. Stir the mixture occasionally.

5 Finally, stir in the fried almonds and serve the dish piping hot.

# POTATOES WITH RED CHILIES

The quantity of red chilies used here may be too fiery for some palates. For a milder version, either seed the chilies or use a roughly chopped red bell pepper instead.

### INGREDIENTS
*12–14 baby new potatoes, peeled and*
*halved if large*
*2 tablespoons vegetable oil*
*½ teaspoon crushed dried red chilies*
*½ teaspoon white cumin seeds*
*½ teaspoon fennel seeds*
*½ teaspoon crushed coriander seeds*
*1 tablespoon salt*
*1 onion, sliced*
*1–4 fresh red chilies, chopped*
*1 tablespoon chopped fresh cilantro*

### SERVES 4

1 Put the new potatoes into a saucepan of boiling salted water and cook for 10–12 minutes, until tender but still firm. Remove from the heat and drain.

2 Heat the oil in a deep frying pan, then turn down the heat to medium. Add the dried chilies, cumin, fennel, and coriander seeds with the salt. Fry for 30–40 seconds.

3 Add the onion. Fry until golden brown. Add the potatoes, fresh chilies, and fresh cilantro. Cover and cook over very low heat for 5–7 minutes. Serve hot.

# SPICY CABBAGE

**A**n excellent accompaniment, this cabbage dish is very versatile and can even be served as a warm side salad or cold with a selection of cold meats. Try red cabbage for a change.

### INGREDIENTS
*4 tablespoons margarine or butter*
*½ teaspoon white cumin seeds*
*3–8 dried red chilies, to taste*
*1 small onion, sliced*
*2½ cups shredded cabbage*
*2 carrots, grated*
*½ teaspoon salt*
*2 tablespoons lemon juice*

SERVES 4

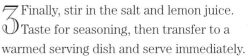

3 Finally, stir in the salt and lemon juice. Taste for seasoning, then transfer to a warmed serving dish and serve immediately.

1 Put the margarine or butter into a saucepan and heat until melted. Add the cumin seeds. Crumble in the dried chilies and fry, stirring, for about 30 seconds.

2 Add the onion to the pan and fry for about 2 minutes. Add the cabbage and carrots and stir-fry for another 5 minutes, or until the cabbage is soft.

# SWEET POTATO AND CARROT SALAD

This salad has a sweet-and-sour flavor, and can be served warm as part of a meal. Offer larger helpings if serving as a main course.

### INGREDIENTS
*1 sweet potato*
*2 carrots, cut into thick diagonal slices*
*3 tomatoes*
*8–10 iceberg lettuce leaves, shredded*
*½ cup canned chick-peas, drained*
*1 tablespoon walnuts, 1 tablespoon*
*golden raisins, and 1 small onion, cut*
*into rings, to garnish*

### FOR THE DRESSING
*1 tablespoon clear honey*
*6 tablespoons plain yogurt*
*½ teaspoon salt*
*1 teaspoon ground black pepper*

*SERVES 4*

---

### COOK'S TIP
Plum tomatoes are the best choice for this recipe as they have a greater ratio of flesh to seeds than most other tomato varieties.

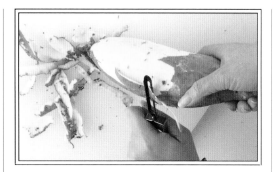

1 Peel the sweet potato and dice it roughly. Put it into a pan of boiling salted water and boil until soft but not mushy. Cover the pan and set aside.

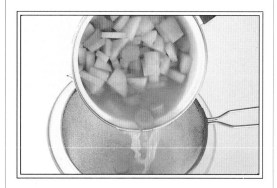

2 Put the carrots into a pan of boiling salted water and cook for just a few minutes, so that they remain crunchy. Add the carrots to the sweet potatoes, drain, and place together in a bowl.

3 Carefully slice the tops off the tomatoes, then scoop out and discard the seeds. Roughly chop the flesh.

4 Line a glass bowl with the shredded lettuce. Mix together the sweet potatoes, carrots, chick-peas, and tomatoes and arrange them in the bowl.

5 To make the dressing, mix together the honey, yogurt, salt, and pepper and beat together with a fork. Garnish the salad with the walnuts, golden raisins and onion rings. Pour the dressing over the salad and toss well. Serve the salad in a separate bowl, if wished.

# SPICED SPINACH AND POTATOES

I ndia has over 18 varieties of spinach. If you have access to an Indian or Chinese store, it is well worth looking out for some of the more unusual varieties.

### INGREDIENTS
*1 pound potatoes*
*4 tablespoons vegetable oil*
*1-inch piece fresh ginger root, grated*
*4 garlic cloves, crushed*
*1 onion, coarsely chopped*
*2 green chilies, chopped*
*2 whole dried red chilies,*
*coarsely broken*
*1 teaspoon cumin seeds*
*1 pound fresh spinach, chopped or*
*8 ounces frozen spinach, thawed*
*and drained*
*salt*
*2 firm tomatoes, peeled and coarsely*
*chopped, to garnish*

*SERVES 4–6*

1 Cut large potatoes into quarters or, if using small new potatoes, leave them whole. Heat the oil in a frying pan and fry the potatoes until brown on all sides. Remove from the pan and set aside.

2 Pour off the excess oil from the pan, leaving 1 tablespoon. Add the ginger, garlic, onion, green and red chilies, and cumin seeds and fry gently until the onion is golden brown.

3 Add the potatoes, season with salt, and stir well. Cook, covered, until the potatoes are tender when pierced with the point of a sharp knife.

4 Add the spinach and stir well to mix with the potatoes. Cook, uncovered, until the spinach is tender and all the excess liquid has evaporated. Garnish with the chopped tomatoes and serve hot.

# CAULIFLOWER WITH COCONUT

I n this dish, the creamy coconut sauce is the perfect contrast to the spiced cauliflower. Serve as a side-dish with roast meats as well as the more traditional Indian dishes.

### INGREDIENTS
*1 tablespoon flour*
*½ cup water*
*1 teaspoon chili powder*
*1 tablespoon ground coriander*
*1 teaspoon ground cumin*
*1 teaspoon mustard powder*
*1 teaspoon ground turmeric*
*4 tablespoons vegetable oil*
*6–8 curry leaves*
*1 teaspoon cumin seeds*
*1 cauliflower, broken into florets*
*¾ cup thick coconut milk*
*juice of 2 lemons*
*salt*
*lime wedges, to garnish*

*SERVES 4–6*

1 Mix the flour with a little of the water to make a smooth paste. Add the chili, coriander, cumin, mustard, turmeric, and salt to taste. Add the remaining water and keep mixing to blend all the ingredients well.

2 Heat the oil in a frying pan and fry the curry leaves and cumin seeds. Add the spice paste and simmer for about 5 minutes. If the sauce has become too thick, add a little hot water.

3 Add the cauliflower and coconut milk. Bring to a boil, cover and simmer until the cauliflower is tender but crunchy. Add the lemon juice, mix well, and serve hot, garnished with lime wedges.

# DRY MOONG DHAL WITH ZUCCHINI

**M**ost dhal dishes tend to be quite liquid but in this one the zucchini provide added body. This is a tasty, colorful accompaniment.

### INGREDIENTS

*1 cup moong dhal or yellow split peas*
*½ teaspoon ground turmeric*
*1¼ cups water*
*4 tablespoons vegetable oil*
*1 large onion, finely sliced*
*2 garlic cloves, crushed*
*2 green chilies, chopped*
*½ teaspoon mustard seeds*
*½ teaspoon cumin seeds*
*¼ teaspoon asafoetida*
*fresh cilantro and mint leaves, chopped*
*6–8 curry leaves*
*½ teaspoon sugar*
*7-ounce can tomatoes, chopped*
*8 ounces zucchini, cut into small pieces*
*4 tablespoons lemon juice*
*salt*

SERVES 4–6

1 Put the moong dhal or split peas and the turmeric into a saucepan, with the measured water. Bring to a boil, then simmer for 20–30 minutes until the dhal is cooked but not mushy. Drain and reserve both the liquid and the dhal.

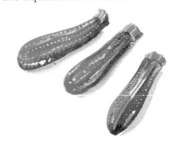

> ### COOK'S TIP
> Moong dhal is a small, teardrop-shaped yellow split lentil. If you can't find moong dhal, use yellow split peas or small red or green lentils instead. Yellow split peas need soaking in water for about 1–2 hours before cooking.

2 Heat the oil in a frying pan, add the onion, garlic, chilies, mustard and cumin seeds, asafoetida, cilantro and mint leaves, curry leaves, sugar, tomatoes, and zucchini. Season with salt, and fry over gentle heat, covered, for 8 minutes until the zucchini are tender but crunchy.

3 Mix the drained dhal and the lemon juice with the zucchini mixture in a saucepan. If the dish is too dry, add a little of the reserved cooking liquid. Reheat, transfer to a warmed serving dish and serve.

# KITCHIRI

This is the Indian original which inspired the classic breakfast dish – kedgeree. Made with basmati rice and small tasty lentils, this makes an ample supper or brunch dish.

### INGREDIENTS
*⅔ cup* masoor dhal *or French green lentils*
*1 onion, chopped*
*1 garlic clove, crushed*
*¼ cup ghee or butter*
*2 tablespoons sunflower oil*
*1¼ cups easy-cook basmati rice*
*2 teaspoons ground coriander*
*2 teaspoons cumin seeds*
*2 cloves*
*3 cardamom pods*
*2 bay leaves*
*1 cinnamon stick*
*4 cups chicken or vegetable broth*
*2 tablespoons tomato paste*
*3 tablespoons chopped fresh cilantro*
*or parsley*
*salt and ground black pepper*

### SERVES 4

1 Soak the dhal or lentils in boiling water for 30 minutes. Drain and boil in fresh water for 10 minutes. Drain and set aside.

2 Fry the onion and garlic in the ghee or butter and oil in a large saucepan for about 5 minutes.

3 Add the rice, stir well to coat the grains, then stir in the coriander, cumin, cloves, cardamom pods, bay leaves, and cinnamon. Cook gently for 1–2 minutes.

4 Add the dhal or lentils, broth, tomato paste, and seasoning. Bring to a boil, then cover and simmer for 20 minutes, until the broth is absorbed and the lentils and rice are just soft. Add the cilantro or parsley, then check the seasoning. Remove the cinnamon stick and bay leaves, and serve.

# LENTILS SEASONED WITH FRIED SPICES

**D**hal is cooked in every house in India in one form or another. Its warming but unassertive flavor and texture enhance almost any meal.

### INGREDIENTS

⅔ cup red split lentils

⅓ cup bengal gram or yellow split peas

4 green chilies

1 teaspoon ground turmeric

1 large onion, sliced

1½ cups water

14-ounce can plum tomatoes, chopped

4 tablespoons vegetable oil

½ teaspoon mustard seeds

½ teaspoon cumin seeds

1 garlic clove, crushed

6 curry leaves

2 dried red chilies, crumbled

¼ teaspoon asafoetida

salt

deep-fried onions and fresh cilantro leaves, to garnish

*SERVES 4–6*

1 Place the lentils, split peas, green chilies, turmeric, onion, and water in a heavy pan and bring to a boil. Simmer, covered, for 30–40 minutes, until the lentils are soft and almost dry.

2 Mash the lentils. When nearly smooth, add salt to taste and the tomatoes and mix well. If necessary, thin with hot water.

3 Heat the oil in a heavy frying pan. Add the mustard and cumin seeds, garlic, curry leaves, red chilies, and asafoetida and fry, stirring, for 2–3 minutes. Pour the spice mixture over the lentils, garnish with deep-fried onions and cilantro, and serve.

47

# APRICOT CHUTNEY

C hutneys are delicious with curries. In India, a good selection of chutneys are often served in tiny bowls to accompany main dishes.

### INGREDIENTS
*3 cups dried apricots, finely diced*
*1 teaspoon garam masala*
*1⅔ cups soft light brown sugar*
*1 teaspoon grated fresh ginger root*
*½ cup golden raisins*
*1 teaspoon salt*
*2 cups malt vinegar*
*1⅔ cups water*

*MAKES ABOUT 1 POUND*

1 Put the apricots, garam masala, sugar, ginger, golden raisins, salt, vinegar, and water into a saucepan and mix together.

2 Bring to a boil, then turn down the heat and simmer for 30–35 minutes, stirring occasionally.

3 When the chutney has thickened to a fairly stiff consistency, transfer to small sterilized glass jars and leave to cool. This chutney should be stored in the fridge.

### COOK'S TIP
For a hotter chutney, you could add up to 1 teaspoon chili powder. Dried peaches may be used instead of dried apricots – or a mixture of the two.

# HOT LIME
# PICKLE

**A** good lime pickle not only enhances any meal, it also increases the appetite and aids digestion. If you cannot find mustard oil, use vegetable oil.

INGREDIENTS
*25 limes*
*8 ounces salt*
*2 ounces ground fenugreek*
*2 ounces mustard powder*
*5 ounces chili powder*
*½ ounce ground turmeric*
*2½ cups mustard oil*
*1 teaspoon asafoetida*
*1 ounce yellow mustard seeds, crushed*

MAKES ABOUT 1 POUND

1 Cut each lime into eight pieces and remove any seeds. Place the limes in a large sterilized heatproof glass bowl. Add the salt and toss well. Cover and leave in a warm place for 1–2 weeks until the limes become soft and turn a dull brown.

2 In a small bowl, mix together the fenugreek, mustard powder, chili powder, and turmeric, add to the limes and turn with a wooden spoon until they are thoroughly coated. Cover and leave to stand in a warm place for another 2–3 days.

3 Heat the oil in a large frying pan and fry the asafoetida and mustard seeds. When the oil reaches smoking point, pour it over the limes. Mix well, cover with a clean dish towel and leave in a warm place for about 1 week before serving.

# SAFFRON AND CARDAMOM RICE

There are two main ways of cooking rice: one in which all the water is absorbed by the rice and the other where the surplus water is drained, getting rid of any starch from the rice. This recipe uses the second method. Try serving it with Spiced Okra with Almonds.

### INGREDIENTS
*2⅔ cups basmati rice*
*3 cups water*
*3 green cardamom pods*
*2 cloves*
*1 teaspoon salt*
*½ teaspoon crushed saffron strands*
*3 tablespoons semi-skim milk*

### SERVES 6

1 Wash the rice at least twice and place it in a saucepan with the water. Add the cardamon, cloves, and salt to the saucepan. Bring to a boil, cover, lower the heat and simmer for about 10 minutes.

2 Meanwhile, place the saffron and milk in a small pan and warm. (Alternatively, put the saffron and milk in a cup and warm for 1 minute in a microwave.)

3 To test whether the rice is ready, use a slotted spoon to lift out a few grains and press them between your index finger and thumb. They should feel soft on the outside but still a little hard in the middle. If the rice is ready, remove the pan from the heat, and carefully drain the rice through a strainer. Rinse out the pan.

4 Return the rice to the pan and pour the saffron and milk over the top. Cover with a tight-fitting lid and place the pan over medium heat for 7–10 minutes.

5 Remove the pan from the heat and leave the rice to stand, still covered, for another 5 minutes before serving.

# TOMATO RICE

his delicious dish can be served as an accompaniment or as a lunch or supper dish. It goes well with fish.

### INGREDIENTS
*2 tablespoons corn oil*
*½ teaspoon onion seeds*
*1 onion, sliced*
*2 tomatoes, peeled and sliced*
*1 orange or yellow bell pepper, seeded and sliced*
*1 teaspoon grated fresh ginger root*
*1 garlic clove, crushed*
*1 teaspoon chili powder*
*2 tablespoons chopped fresh cilantro*
*1 potato, diced*
*1½ tablespoons salt*
*⅓ cup frozen peas*
*2⅓ cups basmati rice, washed*
*3 cups water*

### SERVES 4

1 Heat the oil in a large saucepan and fry the onion seeds for about 30 seconds. Add the sliced onion and fry gently for about 5 minutes until softened.

2 Gradually add the tomatoes, bell pepper, ginger, garlic, chili powder, cilantro, potato, salt, and peas, and stir-fry over medium heat for 5 minutes.

3 Add the rice and stir for about 1 minute, then pour in the water and bring to a boil. Lower the heat to medium, cover, and cook for 12–15 minutes. Leave the rice to stand, covered, for 5 minutes before serving.

### COOK'S TIP
Rice should be cooked in a pan with a tight-fitting lid. This prevents any steam from escaping and ensures that the rice cooks evenly.

# QUICK BASMATI AND NUT PILAF

**L**ight and fragrant basmati rice from the foothills of the Himalayas cooks perfectly using this simple pilaf method. Use your favorite nuts – even unsalted peanuts are good, although almonds or cashews are more exotic, and pistachios add color and flavor.

### INGREDIENTS

*1¼ cups basmati rice*
*1–2 tablespoons sunflower oil*
*1 onion, chopped*
*1 garlic clove, crushed*
*1 large carrot, coarsely grated*
*1 teaspoon cumin seeds*
*2 teaspoons ground coriander*
*2 teaspoons black mustard
seeds (optional)*
*4 cardamom pods*
*1 bay leaf*
*2 cups chicken or vegetable broth or water*
*½ cup unsalted nuts*
*salt and ground black pepper*
*chopped fresh cilantro and fresh cilantro
sprig, to garnish*

*SERVES 4–6*

1 Put the rice in a strainer and wash under cold running water. Transfer the rice to a bowl, add fresh water and soak for about 30 minutes. Drain thoroughly in a strainer.

2 Heat the oil in a large shallow pan, add the onion, garlic and carrot and fry gently for about 5 minutes. Add the rice to the pan with the cumin seeds, ground coriander, black mustard seeds, if using, cardamom pods and bay leaf. Cook for about 1–2 minutes more, stirring the rice and spices, until the rice is thoroughly coated with the spice mixture.

3 Pour in the chicken or vegetable broth or water, and season well. Bring to a boil, cover, lower the heat and simmer very gently for about 10 minutes.

4 Remove the pan from the heat without lifting the lid – this helps the rice to firm up and cook further. Leave to stand for about 5 minutes until small steam holes appear in the center. Discard the cardamom pods and bay leaf.

5 Stir in the nuts and check the seasoning. Sprinkle with chopped cilantro and add a fresh cilantro sprig, to garnish.

# PARATHAS

**P**arathas are a richer, softer, and flakier variation of chapatis, but they require a longer preparation time, so plan your menu well ahead.

## INGREDIENTS
*3 cups* atta *(whole wheat flour), plus extra for dusting*
*½ cup all-purpose flour*
*½ teaspoon salt*
*2 tablespoons ghee*
*water, to mix*
*2 teaspoons ghee, melted*

*MAKES 12–15*

1 Sift the flours and salt into a large bowl. Make a well in the center and add the ghee. Rub in till the mixture resembles bread crumbs. Slowly add enough water to make a soft but pliable dough. Cover and leave to rest for an hour.

2 Divide the dough into 12–15 portions and cover. Roll out each to a 4-inch round. Brush each round with a little of the melted ghee and dust with *atta*. Make a straight cut from the centre to the edge. Lift a cut edge and form the dough into a cone.

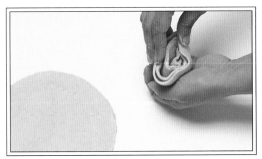

3 Flatten the cone into a ball, then roll out the dough to an 7-inch round. Heat a griddle and cook the parathas one at a time, brushing round the edges with the remaining ghee, until golden brown on each side. Serve hot.

# NAAN BREAD

Traditionally, this flat leavened bread from northern India is baked in a tandoor or clay oven, though broiled naans look just as authentic.

INGREDIENTS

*4 cups flour*

*1 teaspoon baking powder*

*½ teaspoon salt*

*2 teaspoons sugar*

*2 teaspoons fast-rising dried yeast*

*scant 1 cup hand-hot milk*

*⅔ cup plain yogurt, beaten*

*1 egg, beaten*

*4 tablespoons melted ghee*

*flour, for dusting*

*chopped fresh cilantro and onion seeds, to sprinkle*

*ghee, for greasing*

*edible silver sheets, to serve (optional)*

MAKES 6–8

1 Sift the flour, baking powder, and salt into a large bowl. Stir in the sugar and the dried yeast. Make a well in the center and add the milk, plain yogurt, egg, and melted ghee. Gradually incorporate the flour mixture to make a pliable dough.

2 Knead the dough for about 10 minutes. Place in a bowl, cover tightly and keep in a warm place until the dough doubles in size. To test, push a finger into the dough – it should spring back. On a floured surface roll out the dough to a ¼-inch thickness.

3 Preheat the oven to 400°F. Roll out 6–8 slipper-shaped naans, each about 10 × 6 inches tapering to about 2 inches wide. Sprinkle with the cilantro and onion seeds. Bake on greased trays for 10–15 minutes. Serve hot, with silver, if using.

# KULFI

In India *kulfi-wallahs* (ice cream vendors) have always made *kulfi*, and continue to this day, without using modern freezers. *Kulfi* is packed into metal cones sealed with dough and then churned in clay pots until set. This method works extremely well in an ordinary freezer.

### INGREDIENTS

*3 × 14-ounce cans evaporated milk*
*3 egg whites, whisked until peaks form*
*2¼ cups confectioner's sugar*
*1 teaspoon ground cardamom*
*1 tablespoon rose-water*
*1½ cups pistachios, chopped*
*½ cup golden raisins*
*¾ cup slivered almonds*
*1 ounce candied cherries, halved*

*SERVES 4–6*

1 Remove the labels from the cans of evaporated milk and lie the cans in one large, or two small heavy-based saucepans with tight-fitting lids. Fill the pan with water to reach three-quarters of the way up the cans. Bring to the boil, cover the pan, and simmer for about 20 minutes. When cool, remove from the pan and chill for 24 hours.

2 Open the cans and pour the evaporated milk into a large chilled bowl. Whisk until doubled in volume, then fold in the whisked egg whites and the confectioner's sugar.

3 Gently fold in the cardamom, rose-water, pistachios, golden raisins, almonds, and candied cherries. Cover the bowl with plastic wrap and leave in the freezer for 1 hour.

4 Remove the ice cream from the freezer and mix well with a fork to break up any ice crystals that have formed around the edge. Transfer to a freezer container and return to the freezer to freeze completely. Remove the ice cream from the freezer 10 minutes before serving to soften a little. Scoop into a chilled bowl to serve.

# KHEER

**B**oth Muslim and Hindu communities prepare this rice dessert, which is served at mosques and temples. It also features at weddings and banquets.

INGREDIENTS
*1 tablespoon ghee*
*2-inch piece cinnamon stick*
*1 cup soft brown sugar*
*⅔ cup coarsely ground rice*
*5 cups milk*
*1 teaspoon ground cardamom*
*⅓ cup golden raisins*
*¼ cup sliced almonds*
*edible silver sheets, to serve (optional)*

SERVES 4–6

1 In a heavy-based saucepan, melt the ghee, then add the cinnamon stick and sugar and fry for 5–8 minutes until the sugar begins to caramelize. Reduce the heat immediately this happens.

2 Add the rice and half of the milk. Bring to a boil, stirring constantly to prevent the milk boiling over. Reduce the heat and simmer until the rice is cooked, stirring frequently with a wooden spoon.

3 Add the remaining milk, cardamom, golden raisins, and almonds, and leave to simmer until thickened, stirring to prevent the kheer from sticking to the pan. Serve hot or cold, decorated with silver, if using.

# FRUIT SALAD

This is a very appetizing and refreshing salad, with a typically Indian combination of citrus fruits seasoned with salt and pepper. It provides the perfect ending to a large meal.

### INGREDIENTS
*4 ounces seedless green and black grapes*
*8-ounce can mandarin segments, drained*
*2 large oranges, peeled and segmented*
*8-ounce can grapefruit segments, drained*
*1 honeydew melon, scooped into balls*
*½ watermelon, scooped into balls*
*1 mango, peeled and sliced*
*juice of 1 lemon*
*½ teaspoon sugar*
*¼ teaspoon freshly ground cumin seeds*
*salt and ground black pepper*

*SERVES 6*

1 Place the grapes, mandarins, oranges, grapefruit, honeydew and watermelon balls, and mango slices in a large serving bowl and add the lemon juice. Toss gently.

2 In a small bowl, combine the sugar, cumin seeds, and salt and pepper to taste, then sprinkle over the fruit. Mix gently, chill thoroughly, and serve.

# MANGO SORBET WITH MANGO SAUCE

**A**fter a spicy meal, this makes a most refreshing dessert. Mango is said to be one of the most ancient fruits cultivated in India, having been brought by the god Shiva for his wife, Parvathi.

### INGREDIENTS
2 pounds mango pulp
½ teaspoon lemon juice
grated rind of 1 orange and 1 lime
4 egg whites, whisked until peaks form
¼ cup superfine sugar
½ cup heavy cream
⅓ cup confectioner's sugar

*SERVES 4–6*

### COOK'S TIP
To prepare mango pulp, cut each mango lengthwise on both sides of the pit, then slice the remaining mango from the pit. Make a lattice of cuts through each piece, cutting through the flesh but not the skin. Press the skin, so that the mango looks like a hedgehog, then cut the flesh from the skin. Purée in a blender.

1 In a large chilled bowl, mix 15 ounces of the mango pulp with the lemon juice and the orange and lime rind.

2 Gently fold in the egg whites and superfine sugar. Cover with plastic wrap and place in the freezer for at least 1 hour.

3 Remove the mango mixture from the freezer and beat thoroughly. Transfer to a freezer container and freeze fully.

4 To make the sauce, whip the heavy cream with the confectioner's sugar and the remaining mango pulp. Cover the sauce and chill for 24 hours. Remove the sorbet from the freezer 10 minutes before serving so that it softens slightly. Using a spoon or ice cream scoop, transfer individual servings to chilled bowls and top each one with a generous helping of mango sauce.

# VERMICELLI PUDDING

**I**ndian vermicelli, made from wheat, has a much finer texture than the Italian variety. It is readily available from Asian shops as *seviyan.*

### INGREDIENTS
*4 ounces fine vermicelli*
*5 cups water*
*½ teaspoon saffron strands*
*1 tablespoon sugar*
*1 tablespoon each shredded fresh coconut*
*or dried coconut, sliced almonds,*
*chopped pistachios and*
*sugar, to decorate*
*4 tablespoons heavy cream, to*
*serve (optional)*

### SERVES 4

1 Crush the vermicelli in your hands and place in a saucepan. Pour in the water, add the saffron, and bring to a boil. Boil for about 5 minutes.

2 Stir in the sugar and continue cooking until the water has evaporated. Pour through a strainer, if necessary, to remove any excess liquid.

3 Ladle the vermicelli into a serving dish and decorate with the shredded coconut, sliced almonds, chopped pistachios, and sugar. Serve with heavy cream, if wished.

# ORANGES WITH SAFFRON YOGURT

After a hot, spicy curry, a popular Indian pudding is simply sliced juicy oranges sprinkled with a little cinnamon and served with a spoonful of saffron-flavored yogurt.

### INGREDIENTS
*4 large oranges*
*¼ teaspoon ground cinnamon*
*⅔ cup plain yogurt*
*2 teaspoons sugar*
*3–4 saffron strands*
*¼ teaspoon ground ginger*
*1 tablespoon chopped pistachios, toasted*
*fresh lemon balm or mint*
*sprigs, to decorate*

*SERVES 4*

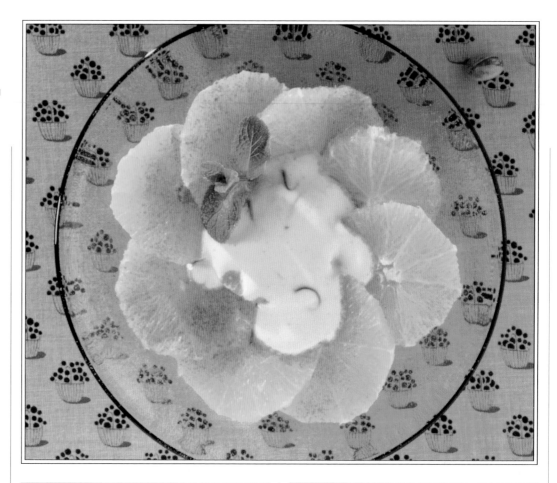

1 Slice the bottoms off the oranges so they sit upright on a board. Working from the top of the oranges, cut across the top and down one side. Follow the contours of the orange to reveal the orange flesh beneath the pith. Repeat until all the rind and pith has been removed, reserving any juice.

---

### COOK'S TIP
Instead of ordinary oranges, try using clementines or blood oranges.

---

2 Slice the oranges thinly and remove any seeds. Place the oranges in a single layer, overlapping the slices, on a shallow serving platter. Sprinkle over the ground cinnamon, then cover and chill until you are ready to serve the dessert.

3 Mix together the yogurt, sugar, saffron, and ginger in a bowl and leave to stand for 5 minutes. Spoon into a serving bowl and sprinkle with the nuts. Spoon a little of the yogurt mixture on to each serving and decorate with lemon balm or mint sprigs.

# INDEX